Racism

What's That Got To Do With Me?

Racism

Antony Lishak

A+

Smart Apple Media

This book has been published in cooperation with Franklin Watts.

Series editor: Adrian Cole, Design: Thomas Keenes,
Art director: Jonathan Hair, Picture researcher: Diana Morris

Acknowledgements:
Bettmann/Corbis: 25l. Bristol Evening Post: 16. Esbin-Anderson/Image Works/Topham: 14. Everett Collection/Rex Features: 11. Chris Gray/Image Works/Topham. Posed by models: 6c & 22. Sally & Richard Greenhill/Alamy: front cover b, back cover b, 6cr, 26. Harper's Weekly 1876: 27. B. Heger/Exile Images: front cover t, back cover t, 4-5, 17. Ralf Finn Hestoft/Corbis: 15. Owen Humpreys/PA. Empics: 1, 2, 7, 31, 32. Andrew Jankunas/Alamy: 8, 28l. Andrew McCafferty/Rex Features: 12, 28c. Popperfoto/Alamy: 21. Rex Features: 19. Roger-Viollet/Topham: 13. Ron Ryan/Cooee Picture Archive: 9. Sipa Press/Rex Features: 24, 29. Topham: 23. Penny Tweedie/Alamy. Posed by model: 20.Peter M Wilson/Alamy: 18. David Young-Wolff/Alamy: 6cl, 10, 28cl.

Published in the United States by Smart Apple Media
2140 Howard Drive West, North Mankato, Minnesota 56003

Library of Congress Cataloging-in-Publication Data

Lishak, Antony.
Racism / by Antony Lishak.
p. cm. — (What's that got to do with me?)
Includes index.
ISBN-13: 978-1-59920-038-5
1. Racism—Juvenile literature. 2. Race discrimination—Juvenile literature. I. Title.

HT1521.L494 2007
305.8—dc22   2006029889

9 8 7 6 5 4 3 2 1

Contents

So what?

As soon as we meet someone new, we categorize them—it's natural. Within seconds, we know if they are male or female and also their age, skin color, height, clothes, hair, and more. It's when we start to make judgments about that person, based on these categories, that problems occur.

What's it all about?

Racism is when a person is judged and then discriminated against because of their skin color, nationality, culture, or religion. Unfortunately, many of us will experience racism in one form or another during our lives. On the following pages, you will hear from a selection of people whose lives have been shaped in different ways by racial prejudice: a soccer fan, a self-confessed racist, someone who was snatched at birth, and a young girl who was caught in a racial dilemma.

Personal accounts

All of the testimonies are true. Some are first-hand accounts, while others are the result of bringing similar experiences together to create a single "voice." Every effort has been made to ensure that they are authentic. To protect identities, a few names have been changed and models have posed for some of the pictures. Wherever possible, permission to use the information has been obtained.

Ask yourself

The testimonies will not tell you all there is to know about racism, that isn't possible. Instead, as you encounter the views of the people featured in this book, think about your own opinions and experiences. This will help you begin to address the question: "Racism—what's that got to do with me?"

Tension over racial discrimination in the United Kingdom (UK) led to this riot in 2001.

An immigrant

When people migrate to a different country, aspects of their home life are different from those of other people in society. It is sometimes hard for children to balance their lives between these two influences.

My name is Sara Wai Hsien Man. My mom and dad are Chinese, but I was born in Australia. Growing up in two communities was difficult at first. My appearance stopped me from feeling 100 percent Australian, and I wasn't completely at home in Chinese surroundings either.

My first big shock was when I went to school—I was the only oriental child there. Not being able to speak a single word of English was very frustrating. Sometimes other children would say hurtful things, but I learned to cope; once I even pretended that I knew some kung fu moves to scare off bullies.

At home, my parents preferred to speak Chinese, while I expressed myself best in English. I couldn't understand why

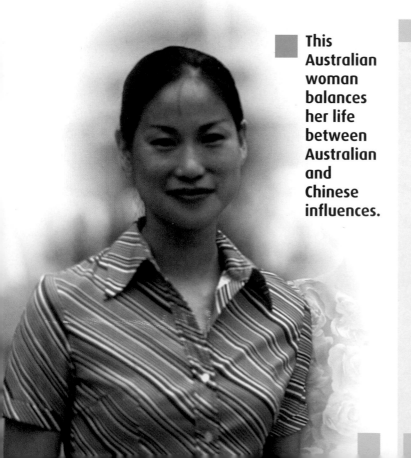

This Australian woman balances her life between Australian and Chinese influences.

Fact bank

■ There are over 30 million people of Chinese origin living outside China. The first Chinese immigrants arrived in Australia in the 1850s. Today there are two "China towns" in Australia where many of the these people settled. Mandarin Chinese is the language spoken at home for over 300,000 people in Australia.

ople in Australia celebrate Chinese New Year.

they made me go to Chinese school on weekends when my friends were outside enjoying themselves. They spent almost every waking hour working and made sure that I always studied hard at school. It puzzled me then, but now I realize that they wanted me to have a better life.

Now I can see how all the new challenges I had to face as a child made me stronger. I have come to celebrate the variety of experiences that have made me the person I am, and I think I have the best of both worlds.

Ask yourself this . . .

■ Why do you think Sara's parents didn't help her "fit in" to the Australian way of life?

■ How could the staff at Sara's school have helped her settle in?

■ Over the generations, how many different cultures have merged to make you and your family the people you are today?

■ Do you think Sara would identify herself as Chinese-Australian or Australian-Chinese? How would you describe your own cultural identity?

A best friend

Adults are supposed to know best. But what happens when you know an adult is wrong? Here's a situation that shows how some peoples' opinions have changed over the generations. What would you do?

My name is Joanne; I am 9 years old. Tizzie is my best friend. We play together a lot, especially after school. Her house is right next to the park, so we play on the swings and then go to her house for dinner. She has a new baby brother named Nathan.

Yesterday was my birthday party. My grandmother came all the way from Scotland to be there. But I wasn't allowed to invite Tizzie. I was very sad because I knew it wouldn't be the same without her. We always go to each other's parties—it's important. At first, Mom said that there wouldn't be enough room because all of my cousins

■ Joanne and Tizzie are best friends.

Fact bank

■ In the past, some people thought it was acceptable for black people to be treated differently from white people. For example, in many places, black people were only allowed access to poorly paid work. In the 1960s, the campaign to secure civil rights for all U.S. citizens was led by Martin Luther King, Jr.

Martin Luther King, Jr. at a civil rights meeting.

were coming to see Grandma. But one extra person wouldn't make a difference! I stayed in my room and cried. My mom came upstairs and said that we could have our own special party after school—just the two of us. But I wanted to see Tizzie on my birthday! Then Mom told me the truth. "It would upset your grandma—she's a bit funny about black people." I didn't know what to say; it didn't make any sense. "Some old people are like that," Mom said.

I got lots of presents, but I didn't really enjoy myself. It was good to have all of the family together, but I missed Tizzie. At school, I told her about what my mom said. She was surprised, but she said that she knows I don't think like that, so we are still best friends.

Ask yourself this . . .

■ If you were Joanne, what would you have said to your mom, your grandma, or to Tizzie? Does respecting your parents always mean you have to accept what they say?

■ Why did Joanne tell Tizzie about the things her mom said?

A soccer fan

Being part of a crowd doesn't stop you from being responsible for your individual actions. At soccer games, verbally abusing black players is still a very public form of racism—but anti-racism campaigns are beginning to change some attitudes.

I was at a soccer game in 1987 when there were men outside with sacks of bananas. They were handing them out to passing spectators. "It's for the monkey," they were saying. They meant John Barnes of the UK; in those days it was quite rare for teams to have black players. I saw quite a few people take them. The idea was to throw the fruit onto the field and make ape-like noises when he got the ball. It was so humiliating. I was standing next to one man who shouted: "Go back to the jungle Barnesy!" Lots of people laughed. I didn't, but I was too frightened to tell him to stop.

I thought things were different now. Most teams have players from all over the world and every club supports anti-racism campaigns—but recently, I heard John Barnes on the radio:

"I don't think the situation has gone away or improved. It's just quieter. If you tell a racist that for 90 minutes on a Saturday they have to keep their mouth shut and the other six days and 22-and-a-half hours they can be a racist, I don't see how that's doing anything to stop it."

John Barnes feels that things haven't really changed.

Fact bank

■ In 1946, American Jackie Robinson became the first black man to play in the previously all-white Major League Baseball (MLB) and was racially abused by some people in the crowd. Today, about 80% of professional basketball players and 66% of professional football players are black, but only 10% of the MLB are black.

■ In the UK, although there are now over 300 black professional soccer players, there are only a few Asian professionals.

Jackie Robinson faced racial abuse from the crowd.

Ask yourself this . . .

■ Just as it takes courage to stand up to a bully, it's difficult to speak out when you see someone else being racist. But if you say nothing, how would your silence be interpreted by the racist and his or her victim?

"Stand up, speak up" wrist bands. These are part of a recent anti-racism campaign.

■ What if one of your friends is racist?

■ How effective do you think anti-racist campaigns like "Stand-up, speak out" really are?

A concerned mother

Most people agree that there should be no racial discrimination in the police force. We should all be treated the same. But as this mother discovered, it doesn't always happen.

If police officers thought that someone was about to commit a crime, they would stop and question them—they might even search them. I have no problem with that. But in my experience, it isn't always what the person is doing that makes the police think that they are up to no good—it's what they look like. I have four sons; my youngest is adopted. They are all grown up now. When they were teenagers, the three older boys were never stopped by the police, but it happened to Darren regularly. He was one of the few black people who lived in our town.

Fact bank

■ In the U.S., the police use "racial profiling" to target specific groups of the community when stopping people. About 32 million black and Hispanic Americans report that they have been victims of such profiling. A British government document, released in July 2004, stated that in the UK: "Black people are six times more likely to be searched by police than white people. There are almost twice as many searches of Asian people than white people."

Many people, like this woman, feel that police officers target people from ethnic minorities unfairly.

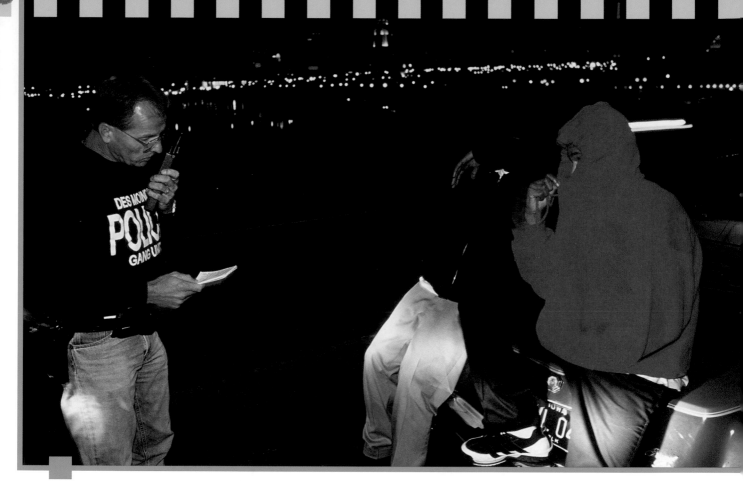

A U.S. police officer assigned to a special gang unit stops a group of youths.

Darren was the only kid who was told by the police to stop riding his skateboard on the pavement. None of his white friends seemed to attract the same attention. One night, when he was putting his bike in the garage, he was approached by two police officers who assumed he was stealing it. When he told them that this was his house, they didn't believe him and started to shout. I was woken by the noise and came outside. We made a complaint to the police and they apologized. But the whole episode made Darren even more distrustful of the police.

Ask yourself this . . .

■ What difference would it have made if the police officers who assumed Darren was stealing the bike were black?

■ What can be done to prevent the police from making similar mistakes?

■ Do you know anyone like Darren who has been the victim of racial discrimination? What happened?

An asylum seeker

Thousands of people escape persecution by fleeing to another country—it's called "seeking asylum." But to stay and be granted asylum, it must be proven that they were in danger, which can take several years. During this time, life for asylum seekers can be very difficult.

Miguel is eight years old. His mother escaped from Colombia in Central America in fear of her life. When Miguel was four, his mother sought asylum in the UK. While she was waiting for her case to be heard, she found a place for him at a local school.

Early one morning, without warning, the police arrived at the house where they were staying. They took them to a detention center from which, they were told, they would be sent back to Columbia. It had a traumatic effect on Miguel.

Here is the letter that his school received a few days later:

mom and son facing return to Colombia

by Simon Forraye

Miguel and his mother were happy in the UK.

Sorry I didn't come to school because I am in the detention center in Gatwick. Well someone rang my door at 6 o'clock in the morning. It was the Home office with 7 police officers and they followed me when I brushed my teeth. I got arrested but without hand cuffs but I didn't do anything wrong.

So they took me to Somerset in a normal car. Then they dropped me off at a police station. And then we waited till a van came. It was a criminal van. It had double doors so no criminals could escape. The van was big...

I am tired now so I will write to you tomorrow. Best wishes Miguel

Fact bank

■ In 2002, 140 countries signed an agreement promising to provide a place of safety—or asylum—for people who are being persecuted on the basis of race, religion, or nationality. Despite this, asylum seekers are often seen as a threat and a burden to the society in which they try to settle. There are about 15 million displaced people in the world—Asia provides asylum for 45% of them, Africa 30%, Europe 19%, and North America 5%.

Asylum seekers are interviewed when they first arrive in a new country.

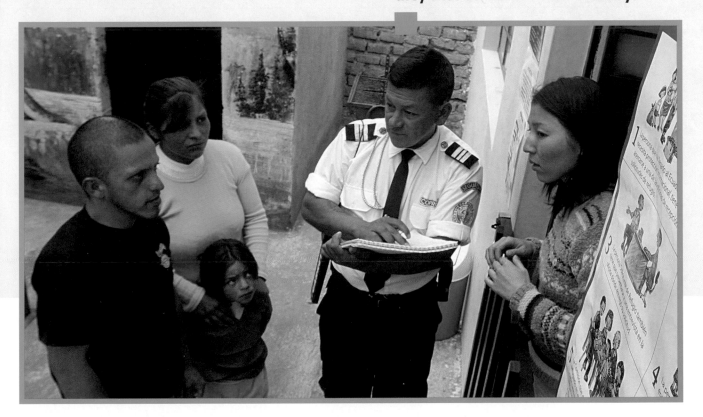

Ask yourself this . . .

■ Is "home" where you were born, where you live, or where your parents come from?

■ How do you think Miguel felt in this situation? Why do you think his letter feels as though it's unfinished?

■ Why do you think some people might feel threatened by asylum seekers?

A Romany gypsy

For centuries, Romany gypsies have maintained their traveling lifestyle in many countries, especially in Europe. Because of their way of life, many other people see Romany gypsies as outsiders. As we hear in this testimony, they still face racial discrimination.

Romany people live a nomadic lifestyle.

"Know them before judging them," that's what the new slogan says. It's on the television, on T-shirts and on baseball caps. I really hope it helps to change things because I am one of "them," a Romany gypsy, or "gitano" as we are called here, in Spain.

I live near Barcelona, but when I visit the city, I am not welcome. Sometimes when I go into a store, they see my dark skin and refuse to serve me. On buses, even though I have a ticket, the

Fact bank

■ The origins of the approximately 12 million Romany people in the world can be traced back to India more than 1,000 years ago. The Romany language has its origins in ancient Punjabi. As Romany people have traveled throughout the centuries, they have adapted to the different cultures they have encountered, but they still lead a distinctive way of life. There are many groups of people who choose to live "nomadic," or traveling, lifestyles; the Romany people are one of these groups.

driver sometimes tells me to get off. The other passengers just stare in silence, but I know inside they are just like the driver. Once, another person stood up for me, but then nearly everyone told her to be quiet and mind her own business.

To me there is a double standard. Everywhere in Barcelona there are the sights and sounds of Flamenco; the music, the art, and the dance [of the Romany people]. It is celebrated as a big part of Spanish culture. I see it as a gift from my people to all of Spain, but it feels as if it has been stolen.

Ask yourself this . . .

■ Why do you think only one person on the bus spoke out? And why do you think others told her to mind her own business?

■ Why do you think some people are nomadic? Should they be encouraged to settle in one place? Why might this cause problems?

■ Why do you think this person feels that his or her culture has been stolen?

Traditionally, Romany people lived in horse-drawn caravans. Now, many travel in large, modern mobile homes like these.

A stolen child

In Australia, before 1970, some Aboriginal children were taken from their families and raised as "white." This is the story of one of the "stolen children."

They took me away to the orphanage when I was a baby. They said my mom was not fit to look after me and didn't even want to know me. It was the same with all of us—they just told us not to even think about our families. They kept telling us we were white. They drummed it into our heads. But we weren't treated like real white kids. My teacher said: "No matter what you learn in class, you'll only be good for serving and scrubbing."

Then one day, a whole group of black women came to the home. They were looking for their children, but they were turned away. So they sneaked into the

This woman was a young child when she was taken to live in a settlement.

Fact bank

■ Between 1900 and 1970, thousands of Aboriginal children were "stolen" from their families and sent to live in state-run "native settlements," where they were taught to ignore their own language and culture. Children were chosen on the basis of skin color, in the belief that lighter "mixed race" hills and we all went to meet them. They said they were our mothers. I thought, "I ain't got a black mother—I'm white." I had become blind to my own color. Then my mother called my name, and I went to her. They had told me she was a terrible monster, but she was beautiful. We hugged and this hot rush from the tip of my toes to the top of my head filled every part of my body. I was 14, and it was the first time I had ever felt love.

That was the last day I saw her alive. When she died, two years later, I was allowed to go to her funeral. I will never forgive them—I was only allowed to see her when she was dead.

Ask yourself this . . .

■ According to the Universal Declaration of Human Rights (a document endorsed by most of the nations of the world), "All human beings are born free and equal in dignity and rights." What do you think this Aboriginal woman would say about that?

■ Do you think that you have equal rights? How can you tell?

■ Why do you think that Aboriginal people want the present Australian government to apologize for what was done in the past?

children could be absorbed into white society. Although this practice is now seen as completely unacceptable, the present Australian government refuses to apologize for the actions of its predecessors.

Aboriginal people at a native settlement.

A racist attitude

There are some people who think that each racial group should live in separate areas and that the more different cultures mix, the weaker they become. Here is the voice of one such person.

I suppose you can call me a racist, but I am also a peaceful white man who just wants to live his life. I don't ask black or Asian people to change their culture; I just don't want anything to do with them. In my ideal world, everyone would live near and work with their own kind of people. I want my grandson to marry a white girl and have white kids that go to a white school. And when they are there, I want them to learn about their own culture.

Look, I don't wish anyone any harm, but I reckon if things carry on the way they are and different races continue mixing together, it's all going to boil over.

Isn't the world big enough for all of us to live in our own countries? I know many people who would gladly buy plane tickets that would send non-white families back to their own lands.

This man would prefer to stay separate from other races.

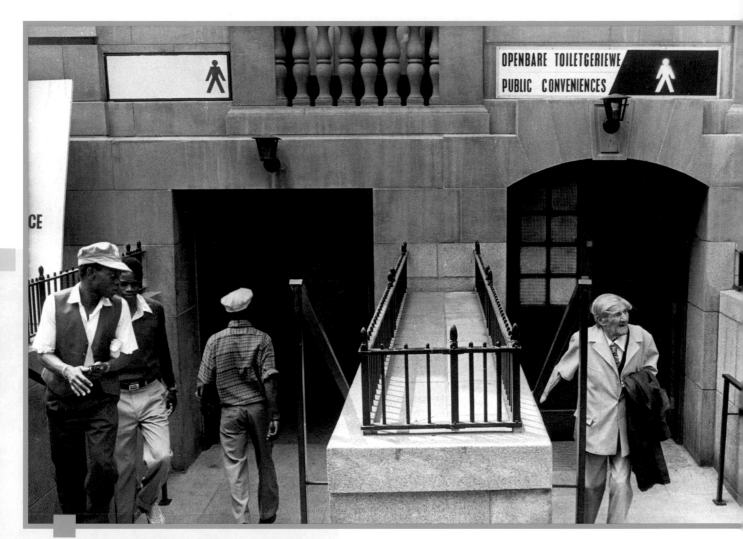

Separate toilets for black and white people in South Africa in the 1980s.

Fact bank

■ The man in the story suggests keeping different races separate. A policy of racial segregation, called apartheid, was adopted by the South African government from 1948–92. White people, despite being in the minority, controlled the government, laws, and many businesses.

■ Today in South Africa, white and black people have equal rights.

Ask yourself this . . .

■ Members of the same ethnic minority group often live in the same area. What effects do you think this has on racial integration?

■ How would your life be affected if this man's "ideal world" became a reality?

■ Why do you think most people find his attitude unacceptable?

A holocaust survivor

History is filled with examples of extreme racist persecution. Attempts have been made to uproot entire ethnic groups and, in some cases, wipe them out. Here, a survivor of the Holocaust (the Nazi's attempt to murder other ethnic groups) remembers her experiences as a child.

I can tell you what happened to me, but I can't tell you why. Of course, it was because I'm a Jew and to be Jewish in Czechoslovakia [now called the Czech Republic]

This woman holds a picture of her taken in a death camp.

in 1939 was very dangerous. But that doesn't explain how people could be so cruel to one another.

When the Nazis came, we were herded into train trucks like cattle and taken away. Just think, one truck crammed with 50 people—no food or drink and one bucket in the middle as a toilet. It was hell—but it was only the beginning.

Fact bank

■ Adolf Hitler's Nazi Party came to power in the early 1930s, when there were over nine million Jews in Europe. In the early 1940s, the Nazis put their "final solution" into action, a policy of "cleansing" Europe

We arrived in a place called Auschwitz—a death camp. We were pushed and kicked and shouted at. Then the selection began. Those who were to live (for now) to one side and those who were to die to the other. That meant the gas chambers—it was the last time I saw my father.

I watched my family die. I saw so many terrible things done by one human being to another that I stopped feeling. Imagine watching someone being shot through the head and feeling nothing.

Ask yourself this . . .

■ The world only discovered the full horrors of the Holocaust after it happened. How do you think racially motivated acts, such as breaking windows in a Jewish-owned shop, can lead to events such as the Holocaust?

■ What do you think this Holocaust survivor would think of the racial hatred that still exists in the world over 60 years after the end of World War II?

Jewish families are herded on to a train car.

of Jews, who Hitler described as "millions of an inferior race that breeds like vermin." By 1945, when Germany lost World War II, six million Jews had been killed—a period now called the Holocaust.

Jews in Nazi Europe were forced to wear yellow stars to mark them as "different."

A playground joker

"Sticks and stones may break my bones but words can never hurt me"—is that true? And what about jokes—can they be hurtful as well? This child thinks about these questions.

I was with my friends on the playground and they were telling jokes. I told one about a man who goes into a pub and says to the barman, "I just heard the best Irish joke ever." And the barman says, "Before you go on, I'm going to warn you that I'm Irish, and so is nearly everyone in this place." So the

Girls share a joke on a playground. Some jokes can cause people offense.

Fact bank

■ Many people feel that if a joke is based on a person's race and is told in an offensive way, it is a form of racial harassment. Racial harassment, like racial discrimination, is against the law.

■ To appear funny, some jokes depend on false racially-based assumptions (such as all Irish people are unintelligent). If these assumptions aren't challenged, they could easily, but wrongly, be seen as true.

A U.S. cartoon c.1870. Do false, racially based assumptions still exist today?

man says, "Okay, then, I'll tell it really slowly."

One of the teachers heard me and scolded me for being racist. I said that it was only a joke, but he said it wasn't funny. He said that jokes like that only make everyone think that all Irish people are stupid.

After school, he gave me a letter to give to my parents asking them to talk to me about using offensive language in school. I don't know what they are going to say. The joke is one of my dad's favorites—and he comes from Ireland!

Ask yourself this . . .

■ What do you think her father will say when he reads the letter? Does the fact that her dad is actually Irish make the joke less offensive?

■ Compare this story with the one on pages 24–25. How do you think racially abusive words could lead to the persecution of an entire race?

■ How much does it matter if a joke is offensive, as long as it is funny?

What does racism have to do with me?

Unfortunately, many people still experience some form of racism—through discrimination, inequality, and harassment. Perhaps you've told a joke that people thought was racist, or you know someone who has been a victim of a racially motivated crime. Even if you're lucky enough not to have direct experience of racism, like the people quoted on these two pages, you will still have opinions about it. To find out more, look at the Web sites. They will also help you answer these questions. Look back through the book, too. Use all this information to form your own opinion about racism.

In your opinion, is racism a big problem in the world today?

"Racism is man's gravest threat to man—the maximum hatred for a minimum of reason."
   —Abraham Joshua Heschel, Jewish teacher, author, and civil rights activist

"The white man is our mortal enemy, and we cannot accept him."
   —Louis Farrakhan, minister and former leader of the Nation of Islam

■ www.myjewishlearning.com
■ www.un.org/WCAR/

Do you always treat everyone the same—even if they share the same view as the man on page 18?

"Yes, I do believe in the inequality of races!"
 —Jean-Marie Le Pen, President of the
  French National Front

"I have fought against white domination, and I have fought against black domination. I have cherished the ideal of a democratic and free society in which all persons live together in harmony and with equal opportunities. It is an ideal, which I hope to live for and to achieve. But if needs be, it is an ideal for which I am prepared to die."
 —Nelson Mandela, former President of
  South Africa

■ www.nelsonmandela.org
■ www.annefrank.org

If you heard a friend make a racist comment, would you react like the soccer fan on page 10?

"If the moderates . . . fail to act now, history will have to record that the greatest tragedy . . . was not the strident clamor of the bad people, but the appalling silence of the good people."
 —Dr. Martin Luther King, Jr., civil rights
  activist and winner of the Nobel Peace
  Prize

"Negroes and whites are different races. We have between us a broader difference than exists between any other two races!"
 —Abraham Lincoln, sixteenth President
  of the United States

■ www.kickitout.org
■ www.nike.com/standupspeakup/

Web sites

The Web sites below feature more information, news articles, and stories that you can use to help form your own opinions. Use the information carefully and consider its source before drawing any conclusions.

www.aclu.org
The Web site of the American Civil Liberties Union. It includes details of current campaigns and legislative updates.

www.civilrights.org
This Web site brings together the work of several different organizations providing up-to-the-minute civil rights news and information.

www.dreamtime.net.au/ indigenous/social.cfm
From the Australian Museum Online, this link about social justice features a wide range of information about Australia's Aboriginal population.

www.civilrightsmuseum.org
Web site of the National Civil Rights Museum in Memphis, TN. Features include online exhibitions and photographs.

www.voicesofcivil rights.org/
This Web site features a wide range of personal accounts and stories from people involved in the struggle for civil rights. It also includes historical information, a timeline, and a gallery.

www.irr.org.uk
Online news articles from the Independent Race Relations News Network.

Glossary

www.un.org/av/photo/ subjects/apartheid.htm
A photo archive of the United Nations Web site that focuses on the years of apartheid in South Africa.

www.romani.org
A Web site dedicated to the recognition of the Romany people. It includes information about their history, music, and dance.

Aboriginal – original inhabitants of Australia.

Apartheid – government policy in South Africa that made racial segregation legal.

Asylum – refuge from suffering and persecution.

Civil rights – laws that aim to ensure freedom and equality for everyone.

Culture – history and traditions that characterize a specific group of people.

Detention center – secure place were asylum seekers are often held.

Dilemma – a tricky and often sensitive problem.

Discrimination – when a person, or group of people, are treated unfairly.

Endorsed – supported.

Ethnic – sharing the same cultural and racial identity.

Flamenco – vibrant dancing and music from Romany gypsy culture.

Gas chambers – rooms in which holocaust victims were murdered.

Hispanic – of Spanish or Latin-American origin.

Nazi Party – political group that ruled Germany from 1933–45.

Nomadic – a lifestyle that involves moving from place to place.

Persecution – when people are treated unjustly.

Racial harassment – when people are abused because of their race.

Racial prejudice – act of discriminating against people because of their race.

Verbal racial abuse – when people are insulted or shouted at because of their race.

Index